W9-ACN-171

Everyday Science Experiments

Bugs in the Garden

Susan Martineau
Illustrated by Leighton Noyes

with thanks to Kathryn Higgins,
Head of Chemistry, Leighton Park School

WINDMILL BOOKS
New York

Published in 2012 by Windmill Books, An Imprint of Rosen Publishing
29 East 21st Street, New York, NY 10010

© 2012 b small publishing ltd
Adaptations to North American Edition © 2012 Windmill Books, An Imprint of Rosen Publishing

Library of Congress Cataloging-in-Publication Data

Martineau, Susan.
Bugs in the garden / by Susan Martineau. — 1st ed.
p. cm. — (Everyday science experiments)
Includes index.
ISBN 978-1-61533-370-7 (library binding) — ISBN 978-1-61533-408-7 (pbk.) —
ISBN 978-1-61533-470-4 (6-pack)
1. Natural history – Experiments – Juvenile literature. 2. Nature study – Juvenile literature.
3. Garden animals – Juvenile literature. 1. Title.
QH55.M37 2012
508.078 – dc22
                                2010052120

Manufactured in the United States of America

CPSIA Compliance Information: Batch #BS2011WM: For Further Information contact Windmill Books, New York, New York at 1-866-478-0556

Contents

How to Be a Scientist

Scientists learn about the world around us by doing experiments. You will learn about the science in your garden or park in this book. You won't need any special equipment for these experiments. They use everyday things you'll probably find at home already. Don't forget to ask a grown-up before using them. Before you begin, always read through the whole experiment to make sure you have everything you will need.

BE SAFE!

Ask a grown-up before you go out into the garden and never go to the park on your own.

Keep a notebook handy. You can draw or write down what happens like a real scientist. You can make up your own experiments, too.

Words to Know
Special science words are explained on page 24.

Wash your hands when you come back inside.

Never eat anything you find in the garden or park. Some plants and berries can be very bad for you.

Quick Quiz answers are on page 24.

Bug Hunt

See what creepy-crawlies you can find living in your garden or in the park. The best time to look for them is in warm weather when these animals are the most active. You might want to wear gloves when you are poking around looking for bugs!

1. Take a notebook, magnifying glass, and pencil out into the garden or park.

Butterfly

2. Choose a small area of flower bed or lawn. Look in the soil, under stones, and in grass.

Spider

3. When you find a bug, draw it in your notebook. Count the legs, wings, and parts of its body. Is it wriggling or crawling?

Worm

Snail

Caterpillar

Centipede

Beetle

Slug

Ant

Beetle

Centipede

Spider

Snail

Slug

Quick Quiz!
What has eight legs and spins a web?

Butterfly

Let's Take a Closer Look!

The proper name for creepy-crawlies is **invertebrates**. This word means animals without backbones. Many, but not all, invertebrates are **insects**. Insects have six legs and three parts to their bodies. An ant is an insect, but worms, snails, and spiders are not.

Caterpillar

Try This!

If you don't know the names of the bugs you've found, you can ask a grown-up or look them up in books. You can find out lots of fascinating facts about these tiny creatures.

Worm

Ant

Quick Warning!

Take a grown-up with you on a bug hunt. (They can carry a drink or a snack for you!) Don't pick up the bugs. They could sting or hurt you! You don't want to risk hurting them either.

Worm Home

You'll need three or four earthworms for this experiment. Look for them in freshly dug soil or under stones and logs. Pick them up carefully so that you don't hurt them. Leave the worm home in a cool, dark place for a few days and watch what the worms do.

1. Ask a grown-up to help cut off the top of a plastic bottle.

2. Put layers of soil and sand in the bottle. Sprinkle with water.

3. Place some leaves and grass on top. Gently add your worms.

4. Tape some dark paper around the bottle. Put it in a cool, dark place.

Let's Take a Closer Look!

The earthworms make tunnels through the soil and sand layers. In the garden, these tunnels help air and water reach the roots of plants. Worms also pull leaves down into the soil. This makes **nutrients**, or food, for plants. Worms help the plants grow well.

Worm Warning! Set your worms free after a few days!

Quick Quiz!

Which garden creature loves to eat worms?

Clue: There's one on this page.

Worm casts are curly piles of soil left behind by worms.

Did You Know?

The largest earthworms in the world live in Australia, South Africa, and South America. They can be up to 10 feet (3 m) long!

Sprouting Beans

Growing things is fun and very easy. Beans, seeds, and nuts are the parts of plants that grow into new plants. It takes a few days to sprout these beans, so be patient! To cover the jar, use a clean piece of fabric.

1. Put a small handful of mung beans in a bowl of cold water for the night.

2. Rinse the beans and drain them in a sieve. Put them into an old jam jar.

3. Cover the jar with a piece of clean fabric. Secure with a rubber band. Leave the jar in a warm place.

4. Uncover the jar and rinse the beans twice a day. Put the fabric back on and drain the beans through it.

Quick Fact

Coconuts are the seeds of palm trees. Their shells are waterproof so that they can float and be carried by the sea.

Did You Know?

Beans, seeds, and nuts are spread around your garden in all sorts of ways so that they can grow into new plants. Some are carried off by the wind. Some seeds inside fruit and berries are spread when birds eat them and then leave them behind in their droppings.

Put the jar on its side so the beans can spread out.

Let's Take a Closer Look!

The beans swell up after their night in cold water. On the second day in the jar, small white sprouts grow out of the beans. This is called **germination**. When the sprouts are ½ to 1 inch (1-2 cm) long, you can rinse and eat them. The beans need light, water, and warmth to grow well.

Plant Power

Plants need water to grow. They take water in through their roots. This experiment shows you how the water moves around plants. Any color food coloring will work for this experiment, but red works really well.

1. Mix some food coloring with water in an old jam jar or plastic cup.

2. Put a stick of celery, with its leaves still on, into the water.

3. Watch and note what happens to the color of the celery over the next two days.

Did You Know?

Plants that grow in very dry places, such as deserts, have to be good at storing water. They have large, juicy stems and leaves. Cacti are plants that can live in places without much rain.

Ouch! Don't sit on that plant!

Let's Take a Closer Look!

Red marks will start to appear on the celery leaves after a few hours. Over the next two days, more and more red will appear on the leaves. Water carries food to all parts of a plant. This experiment shows you how water travels from the roots of a plant all the way up to its leaves.

Quick Fact

Some trees in the rain forest can grow as tall as a twenty-story building. Think of all the water moving around inside them!

Cloud Code

You will need your notebook for this experiment. You are going to keep a cloud diary to see how the different shapes of clouds tell us about the weather. It's like a kind of code in the sky.

1. Go out each day with your notebook and a pencil. Look up into the sky.

2. Draw or write down what the clouds look like. What are their shapes, colors, and sizes?

3. Write down what the weather is like each day and if it changes as the clouds change.

It's freezing cold today.

So the clouds aren't made of wool then?

Let's Take a Closer Look!

Clouds are made of tiny water drops or ice crystals. Cumulus clouds are big and fluffy. White ones mean good weather. Dark ones, called cumulonimbus clouds, bring heavy rain. Stratus clouds are low, gray clouds covering the sky. They often bring light rain. Cirrus clouds are streaky, wispy, and high in the sky. They mean windy weather and maybe storms to come.

Try This!

Ask a grown-up if there is a **thermometer** you can use in the garden or park. A thermometer tells you how warm or cold it is. You can write this in your notebook, too.

Quick Fact

Scientists who study the weather are called **meteorologists**. They give us weather forecasts to tell us what the weather will do next.

Rain Catcher

Make a simple gadget to catch rain and measure how much falls. You'll need an old jar or clear plastic cup with straight sides, a small funnel, and a ruler. Use some sticky tack to fix the funnel in place and keep the wind from blowing it away.

1. Put the funnel into the top of the jar or cup. Place the rain catcher outside in an open space.

2. Check it each day at the same time. Use the ruler to measure how many inches (cm) of rain have fallen.

3. Note the amount of rain each time in your notebook.

4. Empty the jar each time and put it back in the same place.

Quick Quiz!

Can you remember the name given to big, fluffy rain clouds?

Clue: Look back at page 15.

Did You Know?

It's really important to know what the weather is going to be like for lots of people. For example, farmers need to know when it will rain to decide when to plant their crops and to make sure they will grow properly.

Don't waste the water in the catcher. Water the plants!

Let's Take a Closer Look!

Rain falls when the tiny water drops in clouds join up to make bigger ones. They get so big and heavy that they fall to the ground. The Sun heats up water on the ground and turns it into **water vapor**. This rises into the air. As the water vapor goes higher, it starts to cool down and turns back into water drops. These make more clouds and it rains again!

Growing Shadows

If you go outside on a sunny day, you will see that you have a shadow. This is because your body is blocking the light of the Sun. It can't get through you to reach the ground. This experiment will show you what happens to your shadow at different times of the day.

1. Take a friend, your notebook, and a tape measure out into the park or the garden on a sunny morning.

2. Take turns standing still and measuring each other's shadows.

3. Do the same thing in the middle of the day and again in the late afternoon.

4. Write down the measurements in your notebook each time.

Quick Fact

Before there were clocks, shadows were used to tell the time with something called a sundial.

Did You Know?

Sun   Moon   Earth

Moon's shadow on Earth

A special shadow called a solar eclipse happens when the Moon moves between Earth and the Sun. The Moon blocks the light of the Sun and the Moon's shadow falls on a part of Earth.

Let's Take a Closer Look!

When the Sun is low in the sky in the morning and evening, your body blocks out more of its light and your shadow is long. In the middle of the day, the Sun is high in the sky and your body blocks out less light. This makes your shadow shorter.

Quick Warning!

Please remember to take a grown-up with you if you are going to the park.

Rainbow Magic

Did you know that light is really a mixture of different colors? In this experiment you are going to make these different colors appear. Ask a grown-up first before using the hose in the garden. If you you don't have a hose, then perhaps you can find a friend who does.

1. Go out into the garden on a sunny day.

2. Point the hose away from you towards a dark fence or wall.

3. Stand with your back to the Sun and turn on the water.

4. See what colors you can spot in the spray.

Did You Know?

When it is raining and the Sun is shining at the same time, you might be able to spot a rainbow. The colors of a rainbow always appear in the same order: red, orange, yellow, green, blue, indigo, and violet.

Don't spray me. I don't like getting wet!

Quick Quiz!

How many colors are there in a rainbow?

Clue: Count them!

Let's Take a Closer Look!

Light looks white but it is really made of many colors. When the Sun shines through the water spray, the water splits the light into all these colors and we see a rainbow. If you could mix them back together again, this would make white light.

The Sky at Night

You are going to be an astronomer in this experiment. Astronomers are scientists who study the stars. Choose a clear night when the sky is not cloudy. Go out into the dark and look up into the night sky. You will see more if you can get away from streetlights and lights from houses. Make sure to take a grown-up with you.

1. Take a notebook, pencil, and a small flashlight into the garden or park.

2. Find somewhere to sit down and look up into the sky.

3. Write down and draw what you see. If you see patterns in the stars, then draw them.

The Big Dipper

The Southern Cross

Did You Know?
Different patterns of stars have been given names by astronomers. The patterns are called constellations. You might be able to spot the Big Dipper, or Plough, if you live in the northern half of the world. In the southern half, look for the Southern Cross.

Don't mistake an airplane for a star. Airplanes have green and red lights on them.

Quick Quiz
What do we call the force that keeps the Moon going around the Earth instead of just floating off?

Clue: It stops us from floating off the Earth, too.

Let's Take a Closer Look!
The Moon is big and easy to spot. It **orbits**, or goes around, our Earth once every 28 days. You will see different parts of it as it moves around. On a clear night, you will also see thousands of stars twinkling in the sky. Stars are huge balls of very hot gases sending out heat and light.

READ MORE

Krezel, Cindy. *101 Kid-Friendly Plants: Fun Plants and Family Garden Projects*. Chicago: Ball Publishing, 2008.

Slade, Suzanne Buckingham. *Do All Bugs Have Wings? And Other Questions Kids Have About Bugs*. Mankato, Minnesota: Picture Window Books, 2010.

GLOSSARY

germination (jer-muh-NAY-shun) The way in which a seed or spore begins to sprout, or grow.

insects (IN-sekts) Small animals that often have six legs and wings.

invertebrates (in-VER-teh-brets) Animals without backbones.

meteorologists (mee-tee-uh-RAH-luh-jists) People who study the weather.

nutrients (NOO-tree-unts) Food that a living thing needs to live and grow.

orbits (OR-bits) Travels in a circular path.

thermometer (ther-MAH-meh-ter) A tool used to measure temperature.

Quiz Answers

Page 7 – A spider
Page 9 – A bird
Page 17 – Cumulonimbus
Page 21 – Seven
Page 23 – Gravity

INDEX

WEB SITES

For Web resources related to the subject of this book, go to:
www.windmillbooks.com/weblinks and select this book's title.